How to Earn a Six Figure Income with Basketball

No Bs! The best way for players, coaches, and executives to make money in basketball if they are not in the NBA

by

Jamar Johnson

CBL Exposure League
925 W. Baseline Rd.
Suite 105-229
Tempe, AZ 8528

Table of Contents

Failure does not come from losing, failure comes from not trying.
~Larry Brown, Head Coach SMU

Basketball, like all sports, is predicated on the execution of fundamentals. The coach is the teacher and his subject is fundamentals.

~the late Dr. Jack Ramsay, Hall of Fame NBA Coach

The best teams play FOR each other, not WITH each other.
~Jeff Van Gundy, NBA Game Analyst and Former NBA Coach

Confidence comes from being prepared.
~John Wooden, Hall of Fame Coaching Icon

Get the fundamentals down and the level of everything you do will rise.
~Michael Jordan, Owner of the NBA's Charlotte Bobcats & Hall of Fame Player

I want to continue to help my players be successful. You don't just say goodbye at the end of their playing career and end it there.
~Pat Summitt, Hall of Fame Women's Basketball Coach

Once you've done the mental work, there comes a point where you have to throw yourself into the action and put your heart on the line.
~Phil Jackson, NBA World Champion and President of the New York Knicks

I don't complain about playing. My job is to play so well that my coach can't sit me.
~Shane Battier

I have never played in an NBA championship game. I have never played in a regular season NBA game. I have never played in a pre-season NBA game. I have never practiced with an NBA team. I have never received a paycheck from any NBA team. My name was never called in the NBA draft. And after my college career I was never invited to an NBA team workout. Yet, in spite of not accomplishing my goal and dream of playing NBA I have still been able to make hundreds of thousands of dollars in income by way of the game of basketball.

I dedicate this book to every person that has ever dreamed of or is striving to have a career in basketball and desires to earn an income that is worthy of their efforts and commitment.

"Fall in love with the process of becoming the basketball professional that you desire to be."

~Jamar Johnson, Chief CBL Commissioner

Have you ever wanted to have a career in basketball as a player, coach, or staff member? Or thought about what it would be like to own or operate your very own professional basketball team? Well due to advancements in technology and the exposure of the game, career opportunities are flourishing in the adult amateur basketball marketplace and six figure incomes are no longer exclusively limited to the NBA, WNBA, or top college programs. With the national, as well as global interest and passion for basketball increasing annually, now more than ever, is the best time to get involved with an adult amateur professional basketball organization and earn a six figure income for yourself.

For **67.4%** of basketball participants, there is an under developed market in terms of recreational leagues or semi-professional teams. Those reasons include no perceived value in the amateur segment, no scholarship or career incentives to drive financial investment, and no national brands to organize, innovate, and drive this segment.

After players leave high school, college, or the AAU and cannot make it on a professional team, there are almost no professional basketball leagues that operate on a national level. Those that are good enough may be lucky and find a semi-professional team to join, but for the most part the options available are scarce. Because of this lack of an established identity for semi-professional players, those few leagues that are in operation are restricted to their local regional markets.

This market CAN be expanded but it will require the right people with an intuitive mind and the foresight to create and establish the innovation needed to help create this national identity. Once this league DOES becomes established, the growth could be unimaginable. The market for players is there, as we just stated 67.4% of basketball participants fall in this category. And once a league is well-established, it'll prove that there is enough revenue and demand for basketball to draw forth business sponsorships, media coverage, marketing, and branding impacts.

Lucky for you, a new league is here and already paving the road to achieve those goals.

The CBL Exposure League is the premiere adult recreational and semi-pro basketball league that offers an opportunity for players, coaches, front office staff members/executives, and entrepreneurs to build their resume, gain valuable experience, increase their visibility in the basketball and/or sports industry, and to let other sports organizations and leagues know that you are among the best in the basketball/sports industry.

Individuals that take advantage of this opportunity can accelerate their sports career by three to five years. This is not a career opportunity where you go and do meaningless grunt work. The CBL Exposure League opportunity serves as a "proving-grounds and launch-pad" where you can show the sports world that you have what it takes as a sports executive, coach, or player.

While the NBA has established the largest stake in basketball revenue, it is by no means an exclusive domain to earning a six figure income anymore. Basketball is one of the largest industries in not only the United States, but the world. The industry consists of many different aspects – sports tourism, sporting goods (manufacturing and retail), sports apparel, amateur participation (recreational and semi-pro leagues), professional organizations, marketing firms, and sponsorships. With a participation of over 25 million people, basketball is the leading amateur and recreational sport played in the United States.

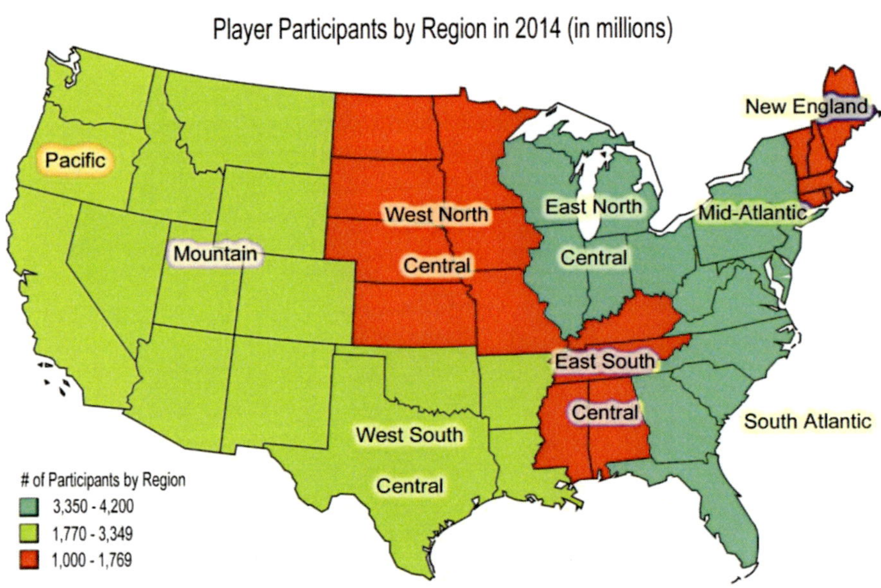

The basketball industry provides a bountiful amount of jobs and careers to choose from. It allows for a person to link their interest in sports with their interest in business, entrepreneurship, coaching, or playing professionally. It's also not limited to just these professions. Someone interested in basketball and medicine can become a medical trainer. A computer software engineer can design programs to help with training regiments and team analytics. A fashion designer can create apparel focused on the basketball market. All of these professions are showing a sharp rise in salary increase because of the popularity of basketball. Below is an example of the salary index of a Scouting Video Assistant.

With the vast spectrum of careers available in the basketball industry, there has also been a correlation at the educational level. Sports management is one of the fastest growing college degree programs today. As such, the sports business industry has experienced exponential growth in a relatively short time frame. The basketball shoe market alone generated $30 billion in 2013.

While it may be promiscuous to think that the youth has the largest participation in the basketball industry, this is just not true. Almost equally representing the 13-17 age group is the 25-34 segment, with the 35-44 age group also following closely behind. This is a vast range of ages to market to, each with their own particular niches. In addition, men and woman participation in basketball in high school has remained consistent over the past five years. With all of these participants, a vast majority will not make it to the professional level.

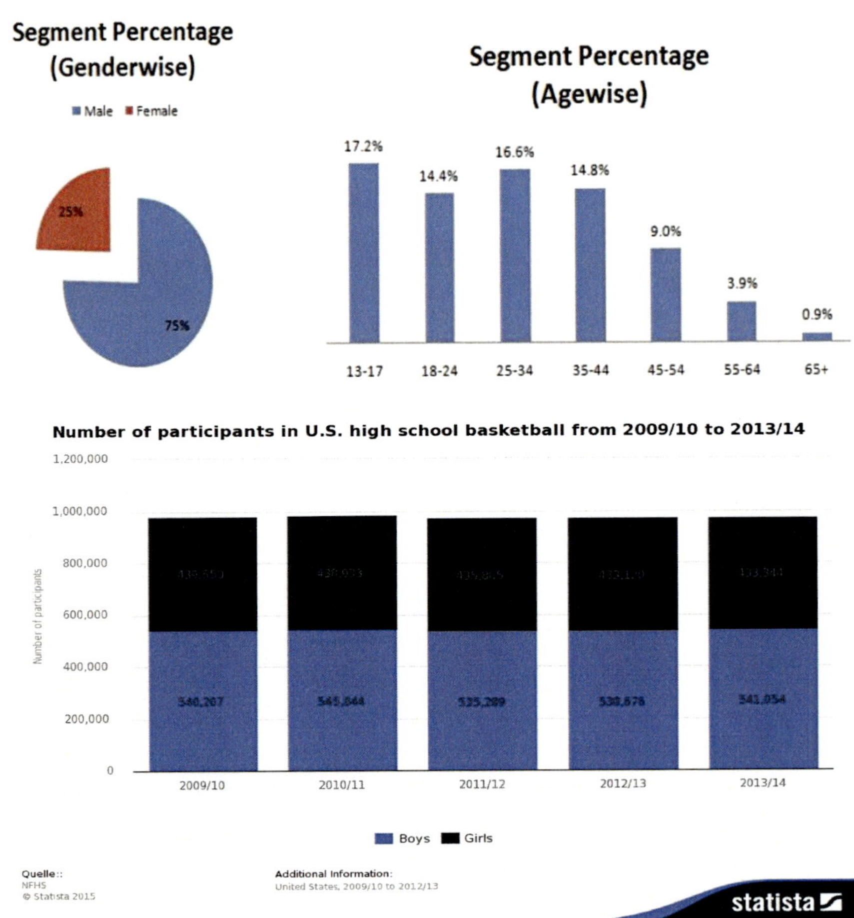

The NBA

To further illustrate the vast popularity of basketball, and a more recent depiction of the NBA's reemerging success, the 2015 NBA finals averaged its largest audience since 1998. With a viewership of 19.9 million people tuning in, it also scored the highest rating since 2001. That constitutes a 28% increase in viewership and a 25% increase in ratings from last year's five-game Spurs/Heat series.

Not only was this the most watched series in basketball since 1998, but it was the most watched in *all* of sports since the 2004 MLB World Series between the Red Sox and Cardinals. It also was only the third NBA finals since 1998 to average more than 18 million viewers and the only NBA finals since 2001 to exceed a rating of 10.0 or higher in each game.

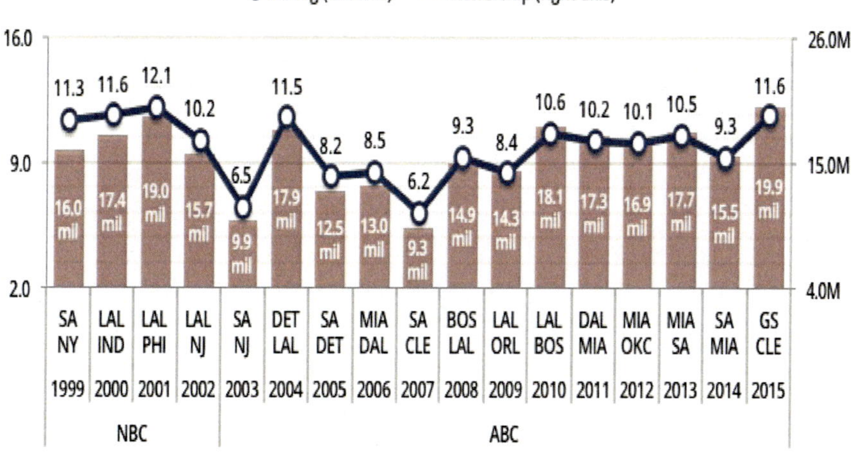

What about the rest of playoffs? When compared to the average viewership, these numbers were also up. All of the second round games averaged a viewership of 6.5 million. The NBA Draft Lottery alone drew in close to 4 million viewers. Game four of the Western Conference Finals alone (between the Houston Rockets and the Golden State Warriors) amassed 9.4 million viewers. That is up a whopping **59%** from 2013's Western Conference Finals (the last time ESPN aired it) and even surpasses the 2014 Western Conference Finals (between San Antonio and Oklahoma City) by 29%.

In addition, the Western Conference Finals averaged a household rating of 5.0. Up 19% from 2013 and 56% from 2014. This just goes to show that people will pay for quality basketball and competitive play.

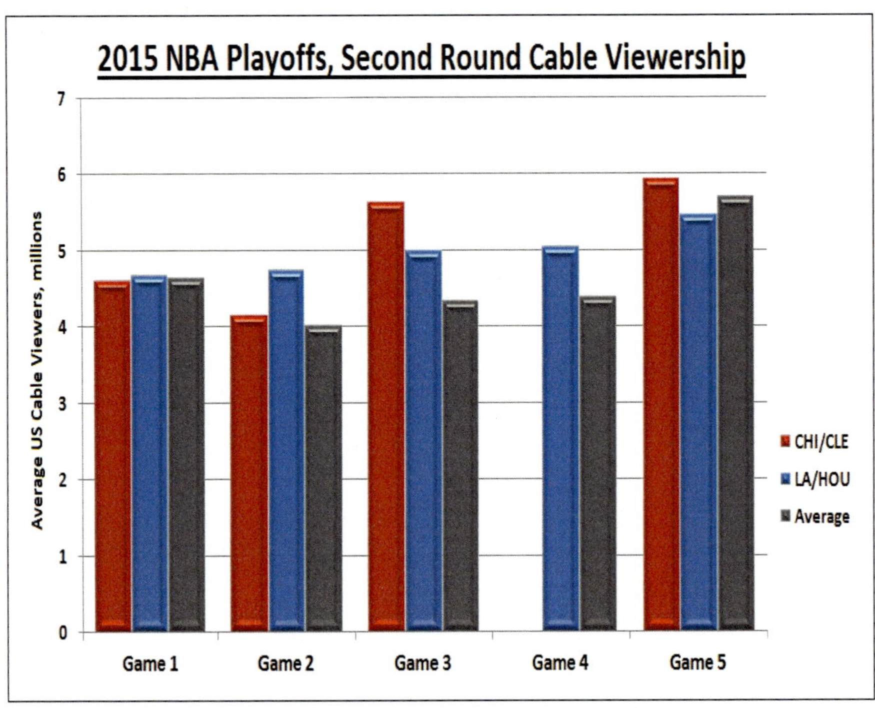

The NCAA Tournament

The NBA isn't the only basketball market that has seen an increase in viewership and ratings. The 2015 NCAA March Madness Tournament also experienced its highest average viewership in more than 22 years. Spanning across the network channels TBS, CBS, TNT, and truTV, the 2015 NCAA tournament averaged 11.3 million total viewers. That's an increase of 8% from last year's average of 10.5 million and the highest average viewership since 1993 (12.7 million).

The 2015 National Championship game in particular (28.3 million viewers) had an increase of 33% from last year's game (21.3 million), becoming the most-viewed championship game since 1997 (Arizona vs. Kentucky – 28.4 million viewers). This is particularly astonishing considering the fact that Duke and Wisconsin, while having a devoted following, are not often associated with drawing in huge viewership. This just goes to enforce the notion that basketball is becoming increasingly popular at all levels.

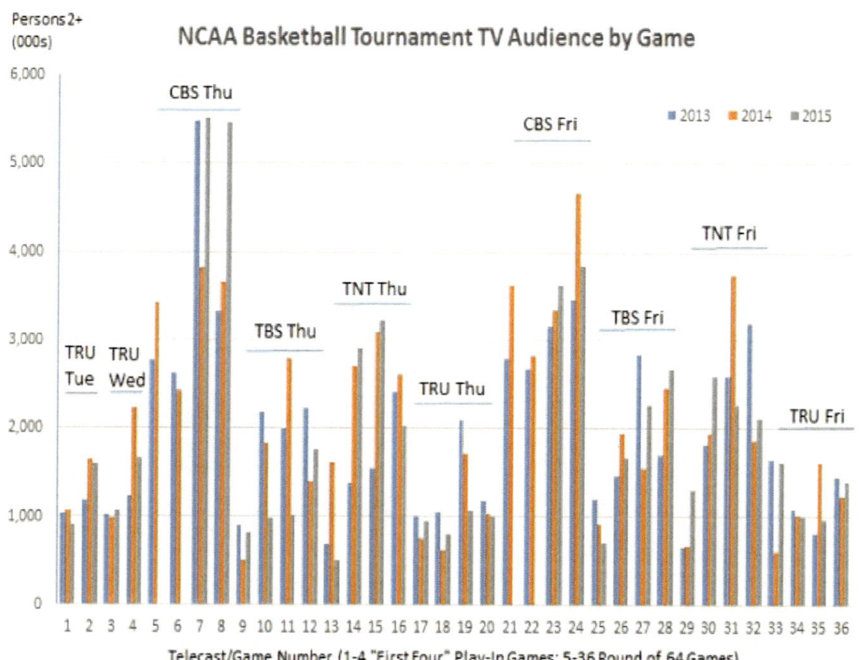

Women's Basketball

Also not to be dismissed is the increasing participation of women in basketball. Women now make up over a quarter of the basketball participants in the United States and has grown in tandem with its men's counterpart. The WNBA's viewership has increased by 86% on NBA TV and 41% on ESPN2 since 2013. Gate receipts have risen by 18% with an increase in 1% of attendance. Even more importantly, merchandise sales have risen by 36%. With this increases in revenue, it's only a matter of time before the trickledown effect reaches the semi-professional level – a largely untapped market.

One can also look at the increase in female college athletes and see how this market has exploded. While male college athletes have steadily grown over the past half a century, female athletes have exponentially grown over the decades. Comparing the number of female athletes in 1970 to male athletes in 1970 shows a huge gap between the two participants. Compare that to the 2010-2011 statistics, and the gap has substantially been narrowed.

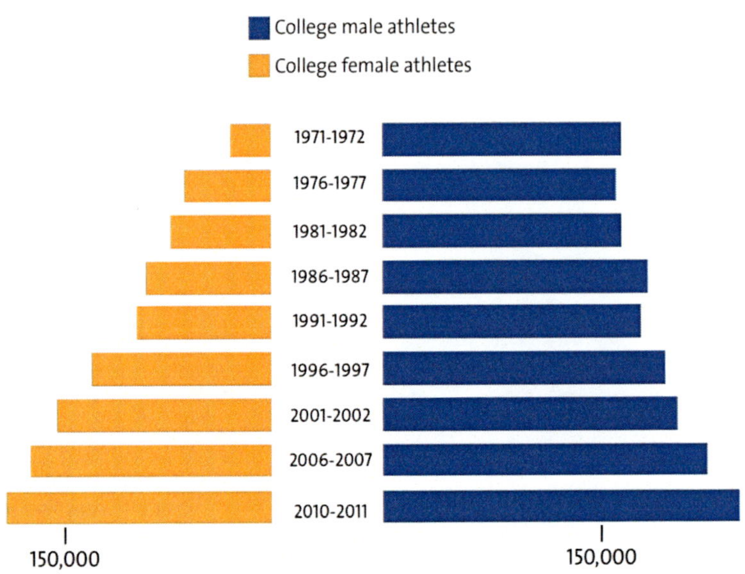

Now that we've statistically analyzed the increase in popularity at both the professional and collegiate level, you can begin to understand the trickle-down effect more. Basketball, at all levels, is exhibiting a surge and demand not matched or seen in the past 20 years. You may now be asking, how does this translate to revenue? For that let's take a look at the revenue of the sports industry, and in particular, the NBA and the NCAA, to paint a clearer picture.

The NBA's Revenue

How lucrative is the NBA exactly? In 2014, the Los Angeles Clippers was sold for a record **$2 billion** dollars. In comparison, around the same time in 2014, the NFL's franchise Buffalo Bills was sold for close to half of that price. So why the drastic difference? It's based on the anticipated market growth and popularity of basketball. When you combine a massive, $24 billion television contract with an ongoing seven year bull market you get an exuberant increase in NBA franchise values.

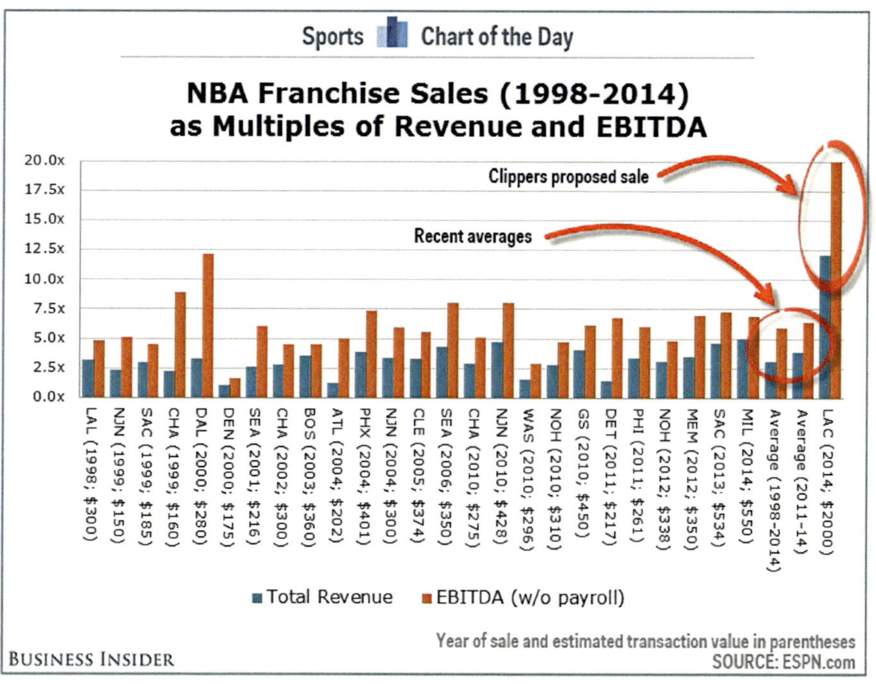

In less than a year, the average price for an NBA franchise rose 74% to $1.1 billion. This was coupled by the fact that even low revenue teams get a bigger piece of the pie now. The new CBA tripled the revenue sharing from $55 million to $232 million. The average NBA team has an operating cost between $23 million and $24 million while average league wide revenue equates to **$160 million** per team per year.

The rise in franchise prices can also be attributed to the rise in sponsorship revenue. In the 2013-2014 season, the NBA generated $679 million in total sponsorship revenue, with Samsung alone contributing $100 million. This was a nearly 5% increase in the overall sponsorship industry. Below are the top eleven sponsors for the NBA and an overview of the sponsorship money increase the NBA has seen in the past five years.

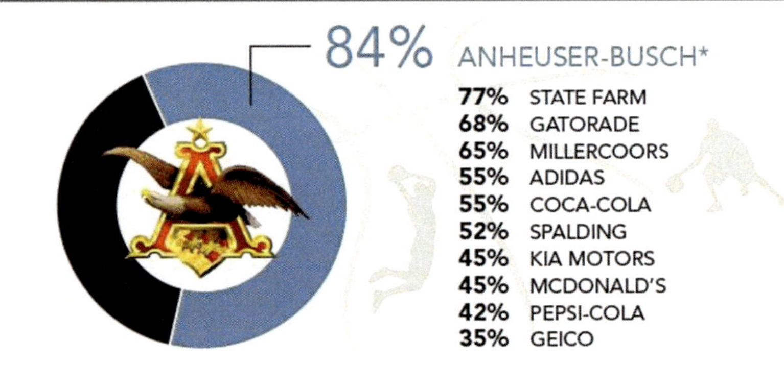

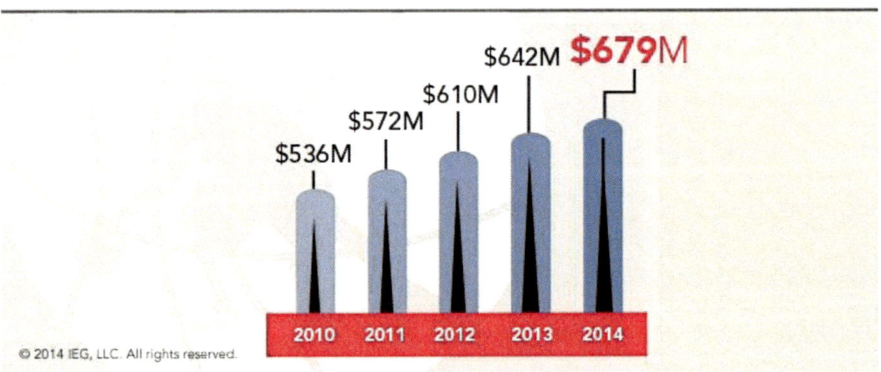

NCAA Men's Basketball Revenue

We can further breakdown the popularity of basketball (and how lucrative it is) by taking a look at where companies invest their money for TV ads. If I were to tell you that basketball was the number one sports association in spendable TV ads you would probably think this had to be the NBA. However, it was in fact the NCAA that claims this throne (further defining the grasp basketball has developed in America). This is followed by the NFL and a close third with the NBA. While all three of these sports leagues generated close to or over $1 billion dollars each, the fourth closest league (the MLB) was nearly $400 million dollars less than the NBA.

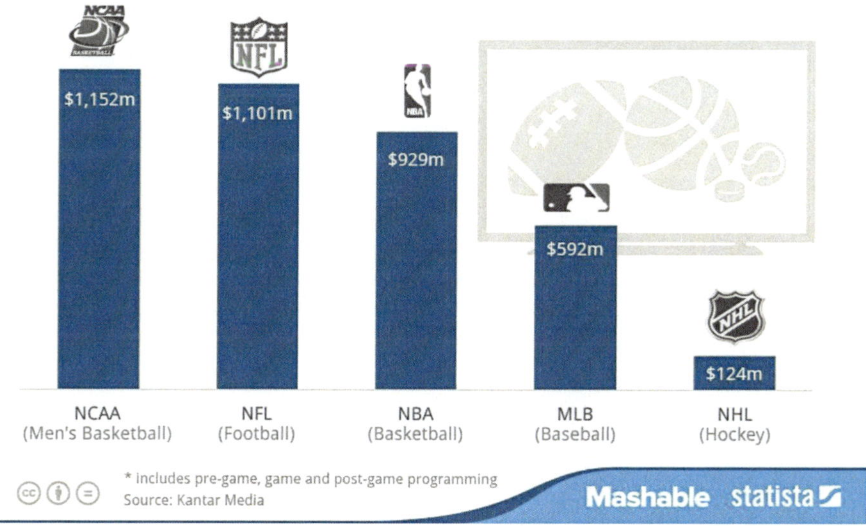

What this all ultimately presents is the manifestation of basketball. If there is this much popularity and revenue at the NCAA and NBA level it can most certainly be replicated in a smaller degree at the semi-pro level. Combined sponsors spent nearly $2 billion dollars in TV ads alone on basketball. The demand is there and the product can be delivered to those visionaries who seize the opportunity.

International Basketball

Another factor not to be ignored is the increasing popularity of basketball worldwide. This past NBA Finals was broadcast in close to 250 countries and over 50 different languages. Internationally, soccer has traditionally reigned supreme but basketball is quickly closing the gap. Such popular international players such as Dirk Nowitzki and Tony Parker are extremely marketable in their home countries. The NBA has experimented with hosting preseason games in Asia and regular season games in Mexico City and London as well.

The NBA recognizes that Asia remains a lucrative frontier. As such, the NBA has invested a substantial amount of time to build their brand in countries such as China. Brands have also began to market their players in China (where Kobe Bryant is one of the most marketable players), such as Nike sending their highest profile players to Asia on promotional tours every offseason.

Last year NBA China (the NBA's relatively new Chinese league) agreed to a partnership with SINA Corporation to establish a streaming service, modeling it after the NBA Inside Stuff. Already there has been an increase in revenue generation in NBA China from this sponsorship deal.

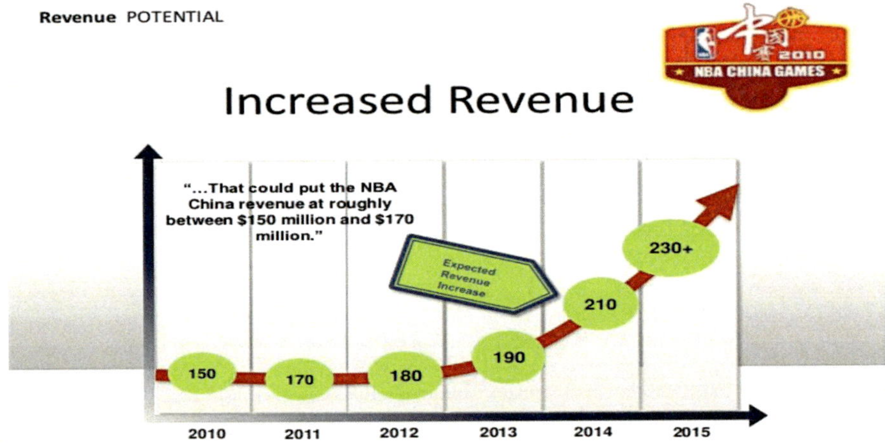

The past 30 years has demonstrated an explosion in sports revenue. One can simply view the amount of money contractual players make now compared to 30 years ago to understand how quickly this industry has grown. While it starts at the professional level, a trickle-down effect is always imminent. This is especially true in the basketball market.

The sports market generates close to **$700 billion** dollars a year globally (including products, health/fitness clubs, and events). We've looked at the different basketball entities, their growing viewership, and the revenue they generate. So how can you get a piece of this? First let's take a closer look at the flow of money.

This flow chart is eventually true for all basketball leagues, both professionally and in the amateur marketplace. While we can see that the flow chart begins with fans and instigates the brands and media, at the center of it all are the leagues and teams. Ticketing, sponsoring, and advertising revenue flow through the league and are then distributed to the teams. Now let's take a look at these different identities.

Sporting Goods and Products

We mentioned earlier that the basketball shoe market generated $30 billion in 2013 but the entire market for sporting goods and products alone is worth $310 billion; this includes apparel, equipment, and footwear. Nike and Adidas, two of more prominent supporters of basketball, had a combined revenue of almost $50 billion in 2013/2014. Below illustrates the steady growth of just sporting goods purchased in the United States over the past 12 years.

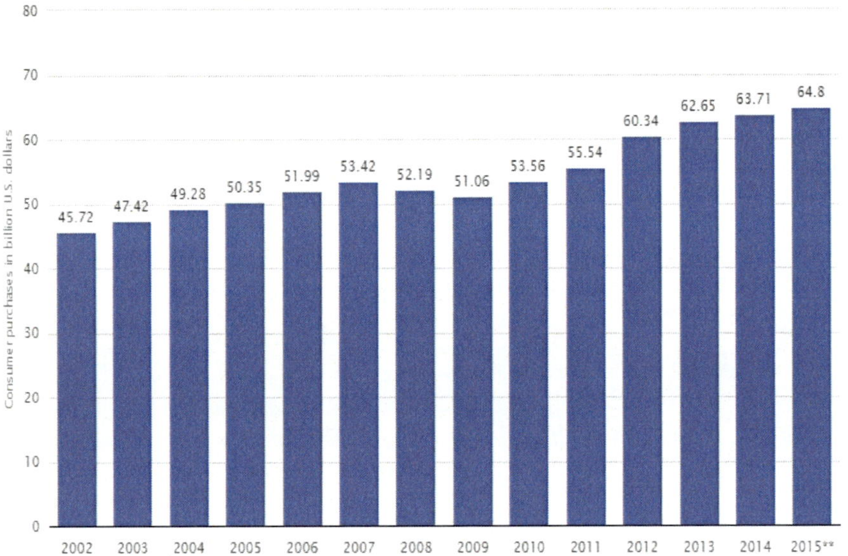

** An estimate of consumer purchases through the end of 2015

It comes as no surprise that North America dominates the overall sports spending market with nearly $266 Billion (Europe generates $204 billion with the rest of the world generating $180 billion).

Sponsorships

In 2014, sponsorships accounted for 35% of sports event revenue with an estimated worth of $50 billion per years. Those brand that select the right leagues, athletes, and teams are the ones that succeed the most in this area. While popularity, price, and the geographical location play an important role for brands, extending their network into untapped locations is crucial. Covering more sports, more leagues, and more players has proven to be a great strategy. Samsung is a perfect example of this, as they have extended their sponsorship into 30 different sports and a multitude of leagues. Below is a breakdown of the various sponsors and their relations to the basketball industry.

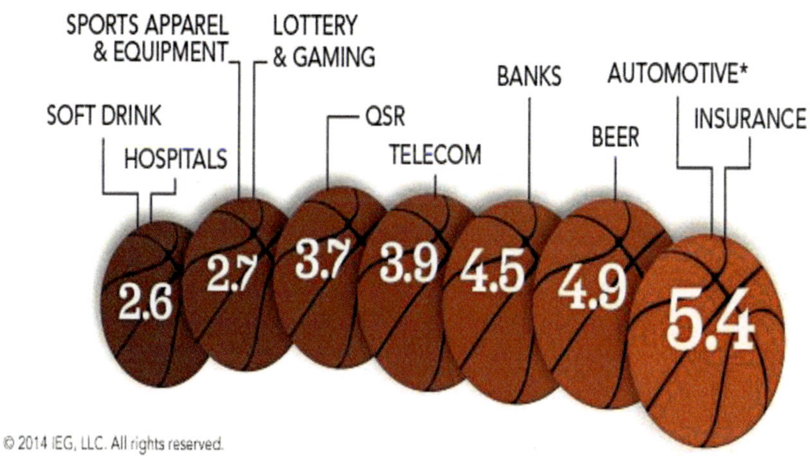

Once sponsorships are established, marketing and media can also be increased. Sponsors want to help promote their products through social and digital media. Creating an emotional connection with the fans and their sports/teams is huge as well. This helps drive inspiration and the sponsor's image, products, and services.

Leagues

Developing sponsors and improving merchandising is a huge part of the business side of basketball. Within the sports ecosystem it is the leagues that develop these sponsors and merchandising while also organizing the teams, seasons, and championships. Leagues organize the competition and help establish these teams. They're also crucial in creating valuable events (such as championship games) that can have significant cash purses.

Like all products, sports is a value that fans want to watch and it's the leagues job to promote and boost those values. They develop defensive strategies such as fair play, good sportsmanship, and adhering to a strong image within the community. They also develop offensive strategies such as compelling competition, revenue generation, and revenue disbursement.

Leagues also are crucial with developing their product through digital and social media avenues. For instance, do you know what the most liked league is on facebook? The NBA, of course. Leagues are paramount in helping to support and generate interest in their teams.

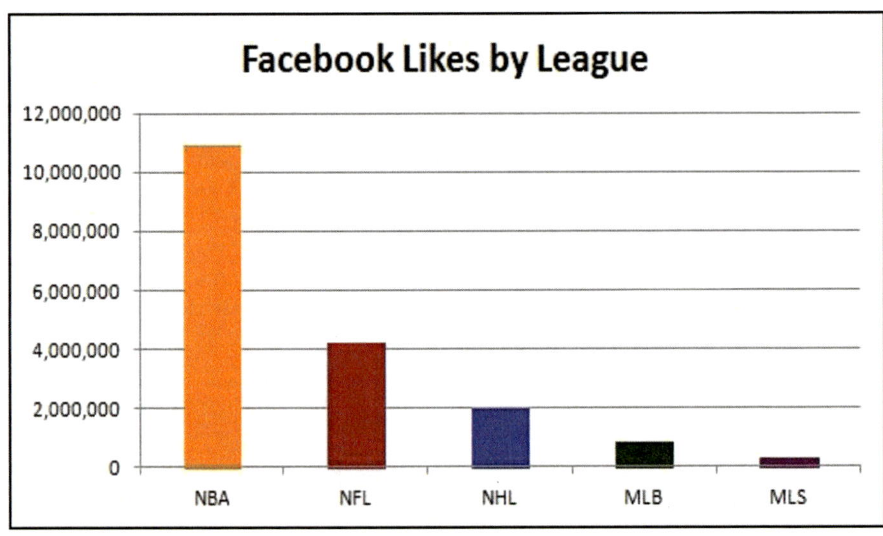

Teams

Teams play a crucial role in the sports ecosystem. They establish the emotional connection and excitement for fans. For team owners, developing a strong asset-building strategy, in conjunction with promoting community involvement, is the quickest way to becoming profitable and making six figures.

Just like the NBA, semi-pro and recreational teams create their revenue from ticketing, merchandising, sponsorships, and media rights. There are three main components that help establish these principles. The first is court performance, or how the teams perform. Spectators want to watch a winning product. The second is individual performance. Being able to market important players can help drive tickets, merchandising, and sponsorships. The last is loyalty. This is essentially getting the community involved and putting them first. Without the community, there is no ticket revenue or popularity.

Various studies have shown that quality production on the court is the best guarantee for generating revenue. While this is the total function of many factors - team composition/chemistry, coaching, and an internal infrastructure - the teams that perform the best, and profit the most, are those that invest the most. Investing isn't just about money though. This includes investing your time, such as creating and finding the right people for your management and coaching team. Or to invest in the necessary infrastructure to find and develop your players. It can also mean investing in the necessary resources, such as manpower, to help with promotion. This in turn will allow teams to capitalize on two major income sources: marketing and ticketing.

People's first impression is that we're simply a basketball league. That's not what we've built. That's not what we've created. What I want people to understand the most about the CBL Exposure League is that this is a platform. We've built this to serve five different identities – the players, individuals interested in coaching, people interested in being front office executives, those interested in sports entrepreneurship, and most importantly, the community and local businesses. We're a platform for businesses to promote their products and services.

Since the inception of the CBL we've been on-boarding players nationwide, getting people in the communities involved, and working to garner business to support us. Then something magical happened.

We had two exhibition games and the community came out in full force. Even better, the players put on an excellent performance with both games going into overtime. The biggest thing we took away from this as a staff – we're ready. This league, the CBL, was ready. The players are ready. The communities are ready. Businesses want to support something positive. Most of all, we're all having fun.

We've designed a basketball league that has never been done before and we're going to bring it to the community like *never before*. This is the ultimate adult amateur semi-pro and recreational basketball experience. It's the CBL. Time to step your **game up**!

<u>How We're Different from Other Leagues</u>

We have a very different business model from the other leagues. We spent a copious amount of time researching and analyzing other leagues, examining what the pro-markets and amateur leagues were doing, and decided we wanted to build something more revolutionary and sustainable. We wanted a league that was easier for teams to get in, for players to get involved, and investing time in those players to allow them to develop. Sometimes it's not a matter of not being good enough and we've strived to make our business model totally different from what's already been established while setting a new precedence.

Anyone with the vision, dedication, and desire to start or be a part of a team in their community with the fast growing adult amateur semi-pro basketball league can. This is the best way to prove to the sports world that you as a player, coach, or staff member/executive have what it takes. Develop your playing career, sports management career, or help businesses in your community.

How Our Team Start-Up Works
Starting a team is easy and, best of all, it comes at no cost to you. Below are the 5 easy steps you can take to start a team today:

1. Submit a GM Application (http://www.cblsemipro.com/start-a-team)
2. Complete the GM Task Checklist
3. Get Team Approval: Begin Operations
4. Submit Team Roster and Game Schedule
5. Begin Playing Games

Our team management program is designed to keep team operational cost low as well. Our research has showed us that this is one of the biggest challenges within semi-pro and minor league basketball. In the CBL, the majority of operational cost for teams will come from insurance ($140 to $160 per game), gym rental fees ($25 to $65 per hour), and game officials/statisticians ($20 to $30 per official/statistician). During the team General Manager orientation meetings we go over how teams can minimize their operational cost to keep their overhead low.

The CBL Exposure League team management program has five revenue generators: Sponsorship, admission/tickets, concession, team apparel (covered in the sections above), and cash prizes from our CBL weekly, quarterly, and national contest. Our weekly tournaments (starting in September 2015) cash prize is $10,000. Our quarterly tournaments (starting in September 2015) cash prize is $100,000. And our national tournament contest (starting in August 2016) will have a grand prize of **$1 MILLION DOLLARS!** Teams are required to qualify for all tournaments. See the Rules and Tournament pages on www.cblsemipro.com for more information.

How to Profit

Below is an example of how our teams can make up to $500,000 dollars.

CBL Team Quarterly Profit-Sharing Plan & Budget		
General Manager	$5,000.00	15.33%
Team Staff Management	$10,000.00	30.65%
Travel	$7,500.00	22.99%
Operations	$9,125.00	27.97%
Marketing	$1,000.00	3.07%
Total	**$32,625.00**	**100.00%**

The following budget is based on teams achieving 100% of their quarterly sponsorship sales goal of $32,625.00.

CBL Team Quarterly Profit-Sharing Plan & Budget

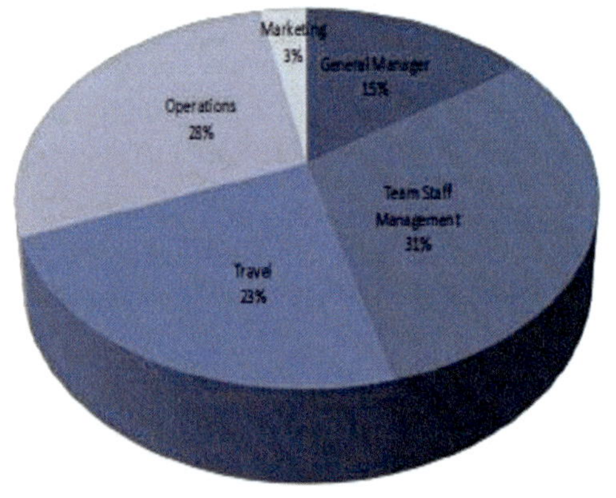

Revenue Categories	Quarterly	Annually
Team Sponsors Revenue Potential	$32,625.00	$130,500.00
Tournament Revenue Potential	$100,000.00	$400,000.00
Total Revenue Potential	**$132,625.00**	**$530,500.00**

** The CBL does not track team "gate" ticket sales. Any profits generated from gate ticket sales is managed by each team's General Managers.

** If a team wins the quarterly tournament, the team's net profit (amount of revenue after expenses) is divide among entire team (GM, Staff, and Players) and paid out equally.

** Players seeking college opportunities can request payment to be made as a scholarship and not a cash payout. Players that receiving cash payout for CBL tournaments will jeopardize your amateur status and college eligibility.

** Teams will be provided with a monthly financial statement for their team every month. Individual payouts are made at the end of the quarter/season. Operating expense payments (travel, gym rental, marketing, etc.) are made during the season.

Monthly Financial Statement Example

SAMPLE

CBL Monthly Team Financial Statement

April 2015 - Q2

Team:	Tempe Top Flight		Current Ticket Credit Count:	0
			Ticket Credits Needed to Make Quarter Tournament:	1500
		Inventory Sold		
Sponsorship Inventory Total:	56	56	Quarterly Sponsorship Inventory Value:	$34,875.00
			Quarterly Tournament Value ($100K-10%):	$90,000.00
% of Sponsorship Inventory Sold:	100.00%		Total Quarterly Earnings Value:	$124,875.00
Quarterly Period:	2nd Quarter April 1st - June 31st			
Total Team Headcount:	31	$3,146.63		

Team Expenses	Budget	Actual
- Operations (26.16%)	$9,123.30	$6,575.00
- Travel (21.5%)	$7,498.13	$2,500.00
- Marketing (2.87%)	$1,000.91	$1,000.00
- General Manager Expense (20.79%)	$7,250.51	$7,250.00
- Team Staff Members (28.67%)	$9,998.66	$10,001.00
Total Team Expenses -	$34,871.51	$27,326.00

Quarterly Team Sponsorship Sales: $34,875.00

Quarterly Team Net Earnings -	$7,545.51
Quarterly Tournament Net Earnings -	$90,000.00
Total Quarterly Team Net Earnings -	$97,545.51

Team Benefactor

United Way of Tempe, AZ

10% of Tournament Cash Prize

Product Id	Product Name	Price	Product Category	# of Product Sold	Total Amount
5	Improving America One Basketball Game at a Time	$9.97	Books	0	$0.00
3	Improving America One Basketball Game at a Time - eBook	$5.97	Books	0	$0.00
64	Player Draft Pool Fee	$25.00	Player Draft	0	$0.00
43	5. Team Slam Dunk Sponsor (3)	$2,000.00	Team Sponsors	3	$6,000.00
41	4. Team Rebounder Sponsor (6)	$1,000.00	Team Sponsors	6	$6,000.00
37	3. Team Assist Sponsor (8)	$750.00	Team Sponsors	8	$6,000.00
35	1. Community Team Sponsor (24)	$375.00	Team Sponsors	24	$9,000.00
31	2. Team Backcourt Sponsor (15)	$525.00	Team Sponsors	15	$7,875.00
25	5. CBL Super Fan	$300.00	Ticket Credits	0	$0.00
19	4. CBL Fabulous Fan	$150.00	Ticket Credits	0	$0.00
15	3. CBL Fan	$75.00	Ticket Credits	0	$0.00
7	2. Season Ticket Credit	$40.00	Ticket Credits	0	$0.00
1	1. Individual Ticket Credit	$5.00	Ticket Credits	0	$0.00
66	iNeedponor$hip Toolkit: Do-It-Yourself	$497.97	Toolkits	0	$0.00
54	Sponsorship Package: Done For You	$1,997.97	Toolkits	0	$0.00
49	iNeedponor$hip Toolkit: Online Workshop & Coaching	$997.97	Toolkits	0	$0.00
17	Get Scouted and Recruited: College Edition	$74.99	Toolkits	0	$0.00
			Total Quarterly Sales -	56	$34,875.00

CBL Team Levels

CBL Exposure League Team Levels: May 1st, 2015

Team Levels	Community Team	Semi-Pro Team	Pro Team
League Registration Fee	$0.00	$0.00	$0.00
Team Staff Requirement	GM + 1	GM + 5	GM + 10 (All Positions Staffed)
Percentage of Sold Ads on Team Website	0%	50%	100%
National Champion Cash Prize - 2015**	$10,000.00	Up to $50,000.00	Up to $100,000.00
Number of Teams Allowed Per City	Unlimited	Unlimited	Unlimited
Full Team Roster	20 Players Max	20 Players Max	20 Players Max
Games Allowed	30 Official Games	60 Official Games	120 Official Games
Quarterly Shootout Qualifier: Required Ticket Credits	500	1000	1500
Qualify for Team Awards	★	★	★
Player Statistics Tracking	★	★	★
Game Scheduling Support	★	★	★
Branded Team Website	★	★	★
Official Online Team Store	n/a	n/a	★
National Cover Story Press Release	n/a	n/a	★
Shootout Qualifier: Required Games Played	15	15	15
Final Four Qualifier: Required Games Played	60	60	60
10% Community Benefactor: Required	Non-Profit or Business	Non-Profit or Business	Non-Profit or Business
CBL Player Draft Pool Fee	See Play Page	See Play Page	See Play Page

CBL Tournament Rules and Earning Potential:

All teams must use the Official CBL Statistics application for all games.
72 teams can qualify for our tournaments.
Teams are seeded by ticket credit amounts (i.e. highest ticket credits #1 seed).
All quarterly or national tournaments will be single game elimination.
Each quarterly Shootout Tournament is $100K if 72 teams make qualification requirements.
Each team's website advertisement space is worth $32,625.00 per quarter ($130,500.00 annually).

Total annual team earnings potential is **$530,500.00.**

START A TEAM AT WWW.CBLSEMIPRO.COM/START-A-TEAM

CBL
CBL Exposure League

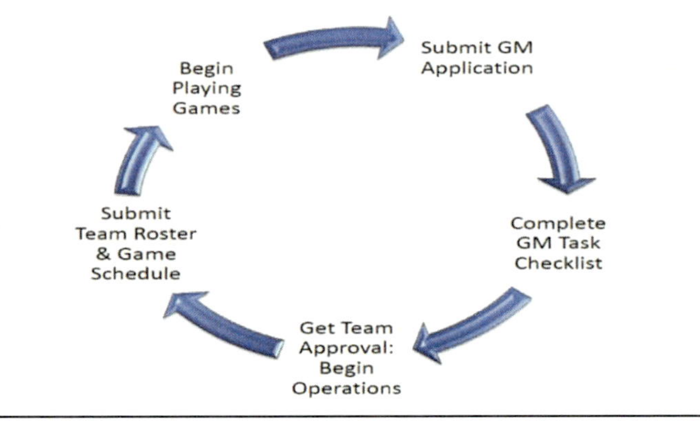

Purchasing Tickets

Individual Game Ticket Credits
Purchase game tickets at http://www.cblsemipro.com/get-tickets

- $5.00 pp during pre and regular season (May thru July)
- $10.00 pp during the playoffs season (August)
- "Ticket Credits" helps teams achieve their Team Awards.

Season Ticket Credits
Purchase season tickets at http://www.cblsemipro.com/get-tickets

- $40.00 pp during post and pre-season (September thru April)
- $75.00 pp for regular season (May 1st – 31st)
- "Ticket Credits" helps teams achieve their Team Awards.

* *You will be able to select the team/city after you checkout.*

SUPPORT A TEAM NOW!
Here's how the ticket credits works…
1. Fans select and purchase their ticket package.
2. Fans will be emailed a link to select the location for their tickets.
4. Fans ticket credits will be added to the team. You will be contacted by the CBL corporate office if you purchased a branding and marketing package for a team.

Why are all of these statistics and facts so important for someone interested in pursuing a career in the basketball industry? Simply put, it helps define the endless possibilities (and revenue) of the sports industry of basketball. It provides an overview of the different products, businesses, and aspects that compromise the basketball industry. It also sheds insight on the different groups of consumers; not only the end consumers but also the business consumers.

Sports will continue to expand and grow into niche markets as long as the valuable parts are there. The media and entertainment industry will also help power this global growth for years to come. As we continue to advance in a digitally dominant world, where social media has been paired with smart devices, sports will continue to evolve. Significant growth opportunities are now present and products can be shared instantaneously and from anywhere in the world.

Someone who just gradually looks at basketball would surmise that it's a competitive sport that can be highly entertaining. Someone with a business mind that looks at basketball sees the goods, services, people, and ideas that make the sport so popular – and profitable.

Those who love the game of basketball and desire to earn an income from the game will soon realize that six figure income opportunities are not just restricted to the top echelon of the sports industry. I have a vision to create an economy in the adult amateur basketball space never before seen. I believe that if you truly love the game of basketball you should have the right to earning a living from it. I see the future of this economy and this is why I have taken action and made this a reality. While there are still strategic and operational challenges that must be met and conquered, the future looks very bright because our league registration for players and teams continues to sky rocket. I hope you become a part of our league and help us usher in a new era in adult amateur and semi-pro basketball.

To get involved today and start making money while working on something you're passionate about. Visit http://www.cblsemipro.com/ for more information.

Be a part of ushering in a new era in basketball history!

Profile Q&A with Jamar Johnson
Chief Commissioner of the Community Basketball Leagues

What is the CBL?

The Community Basketball Leagues (CBL) is a professional basketball organization and network for amateur players.

Where is the CBL?

The CBL is based in Tempe, AZ and we have teams all across the United States. We start teams wherever there is pre-paid player, team owner, or community demand. We have over 600 CBL team/city locations nationwide that we can start a team in.

What makes the CBL special?

What makes the CBL special is the fact that we didn't create another recreational or semi-pro basketball league. We created a basketball platform where anyone in the community can benefit, prosper, or profit from. The CBL isn't just about basketball. The CBL is about improving people, communities, and businesses and our business model proves it.

What was the best and worst thing that's happened to the CBL?

The first year of our league we had a All-Star weekend event and we sold over 5,000 tickets that weekend and I entrusted the wrong person to secure the money and most of it came up missing. This incident caused a serious financial hardship for the second half of the season that year and almost put the CBL out of business. Looking back five years later, the best thing that happened is that I didn't give up after that incident. I'm glad I found a way to stay in business.

What was the lesson you learned from that incident as a business owner?

I try to totally stay away from doing cash transactions unless I absolutely have to. Now we do 99.9% of our sales transaction via online and credit cards. It also makes for easier record keeping and information tracking with our business.

What gets you excited to go to work every day?

I truly believe that the CBL is a game-changer. One day soon the CBL will have players playing in the NBA. One of our team owners is going to make half a million dollars. And several of our sponsors are going to have record breaking sales years because they have partnered with us. This is what has me so excited. Hell, some days I don't even want to stop working!

Last, what advice would you give about becoming successful to someone?

The first thing I would say is don't let others determine what your success is suppose to be for you. A lot of people that knew me growing up might think that I'm not successful because I didn't make it to the NBA, but my goal ever since my freshman year in college was to have my own business. Second, I would say be prepared to make some sacrifices that will impact you on a personal level. Third, fall in love with the process of becoming successful and great. Embrace your trails and celebrate the small stuff because it will help you with maintaining your sanity.

Jamar Johnson is the Chief CBL Commissioner and author of Improving America One Basketball Game at a Time. For more information about the Community Basketball Leagues go to www.CBLsemipro.com and www.CBLHOOPSUSA.com.

When it's time to go to the next level... *YOU NEED TO* START HERE!

No one becomes a success in anything on their own and we all need access to individuals and things that can help us unlock our breakthrough. This is the real power behind successful people and organizations.

As a former college and professional basketball player, entrepreneur, and author, Jamar has always been a performance and results driven person. He understands what it takes to be successful in sports, business, and with people. Jamar has a unique ability to fully engage with people and organizations and create high energy, teamwork, and goal attainment!

Speaking Topics Include:

- Overcoming your obstacles is ***EASY***: When you know your "Why"
- It's never about the organization: It's "always" about the ***TEAM!***
- Transition into being ***DYNAMIC***: Work, lead, and play with passion
- Stop sabotaging your own success: There's no need to be a ***COWARD!***
- Customer service is ***DEAD!***: Start giving customers an experience with your brand

For more detailed description of these topics, see page 2.

When you're looking for a speaker to help you Inspire, Equip, and Improve your audience you definitely need to book **JAMAR JOHNSON**!

Take your organization,team, or audience to the **Next Level** both **personally** and **professionally.**

www.jamarjohnson.com
me@jamarjohnson.com
925 W. Baseline Rd.
Suite 105-229
Tempe, AZ 85283
O/F) 1-855-386-5225

JAMAR JOHNSON

SPEAKER, AUTHOR, BUSINESS LEADER

Jamar Johnson Speaks on the thoughts that resonates within the minds of business leaders and individuals that strive to be top performers. Audiences Love, Enjoy, and Learn with Jamar Johnson!

Made in the USA
San Bernardino, CA
03 August 2016